THE LION NEVER SLEEPS

THE LION NEVER SLEEPS

PREPARING THOSE YOU LOVE
FOR SATAN'S ATTACKS

MIKE TALIAFERRO

DPI

**DISCIPLESHIP
PUBLICATIONS
INTERNATIONAL**

One Merrill Street
Woburn, MA 01801
1(800)727-8273   Fax (617)937-3889

The Lion Never Sleeps

©1996 by Discipleship Publications International
One Merrill Street, Woburn, MA 01801

Printed in the United States of America

Book design and cover illustration
by Chris Costello

ISBN 1-884553-78-8

Dedication

I first met Steve Johnson in 1982 in Boston, Massachusetts. I was a recent college graduate who knew virtually nothing about the ministry. Steve was the associate minister for the fastest growing church in America at that time. Why he took me under his wing, I'll never know, but fourteen years later I am still thanking God daily for his discipling of me.

In 1983 Steve and his wife, Lisa, led a church planting to New York City. We had the opportunity to be tutored by "the expert builders," and it totally changed our lives. The congregation has now grown to an attendance of almost 10,000. Since then we've lived in six different countries, trying our hardest to imitate what we learned in New York and what we continue to learn, as well.

Steve has been my friend, mentor and confidante for fourteen years now. I thank God that we work together. I look forward to many years ahead of following his lead. In my heart, Steve Johnson is the standard by which excellence is measured, and I joyfully dedicate this book to him.

Contents

Be self-controlled and alert. Your enemy the devil prowls around like a roaring lion looking for someone to devour.

1 Peter 5:8

CHAPTER ONE

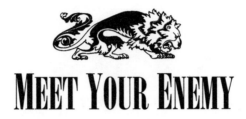

MEET YOUR ENEMY

*The lion has roared—
who will not fear?*

AMOS 3:8

The dark night sky was slowly brightening into a crimson sunrise, and light began creeping over a cool eastern horizon. It was going to be another clear South African morning. Somewhere near the Mozambican border, a zebra stood perfectly motionless, peering into the forest. Something seemed strange. The wind was at her back, and she saw nothing unusual. Yet something was not right.

Earlier she had been with the herd as they grazed in the meadow. She felt secure in their number. The grass was good and the air was cool. She hardly noticed that her companions had moved on. Just a bit more to eat, and she would go too. But then she heard something. A small branch cracking, or a funny rustling of the grass.

Hardly noticeable to a human, the strange noise was like an alarm siren to the zebra. Fear gripped her as she realized she was being watched. But she did not know which way to run, and who or how many were out there. She was very anxious, and it took all her self-control to remain motionless. She stood like a statue for twenty minutes.

In the tall grass two eyes stared coldly at the zebra. The lioness was hungry, yet cautious. It had been several days since she had eaten, but she knew it was not yet time. She peered through the grass, crouching low, tail down, chin near the ground, waiting. On her far left and right were two other lionesses inching unseen toward the zebra; soon they would be in position. Behind the huntresses were the male and the cubs; the 450-pound male had chosen not to hunt that morning.

A few meters away, the zebra faltered. The fear of being alone surpassed the fear of some unknown beast in the grass. She turned slowly and began to move deliberately toward the herd. Ever alert, she unknowingly turned her back to the leading lioness.

Seizing the moment, the lioness moved forward through the grass. Totally camouflaged, she moved quickly with her head and tail low, still in a crouched position.

Then the zebra heard it: a horrifying roar, a loud, terrifying sound that she could actually feel. Its purpose was to intimidate her, and it succeeded. The zebra was spooked and quickly turned her head in fright. She glanced into the grass for a split second before she spotted the charging beast. She turned and ran. But it was too late. Once moving, a lion can cover the length of a basketball court in just over one second.

The first lioness slammed into the zebra at shoulder height, sending both animals tumbling in a cloud of dust and grass. Losing all sense of direction, the panicked zebra struggled to get back on her feet. Streaking through the air came the paw of the second lioness, who had charged close behind the first. As the razor-sharp two-inch-long talons sliced through the zebra's skin and neck muscles, the force of the blow knocked her off balance again. As she fell backward, the first lioness bit down hard on the her neck. With its teeth sinking in deeply, the beast crushed her windpipe as if she were caught in a vise grip. The zebra struggled to move, but the lioness' hold on her neck was unbreakable. She would be unconscious in a moment, but the lions did not wait. Hunger spurred them on as they ripped into the zebra's bowels. Indeed, her last experience of life would be the excruciating pain of being eaten alive. The zebra lay there stunned and dying, the pain of suffocation exceeded only by the agony of her flesh being torn apart. Soon the light faded from her eyes entirely.

Now the entire pride gathered. The male, as well as his three female partners, situated themselves at the key positions for devouring their meal. The little cubs pushed to eat but they would eat only after the adults were full.

In the grass a hundred meters away, some hyenas watched closely. They knew the sun's heat would drive the lions into the shade later in the day. They waited for a chance to steal some choice body parts. Vultures, too, began to hover.

But in this game park another animal soon approached. His vehicle could be heard, seen and smelled as many as two kilometers away. It came, clumsily bounding over the ground, belching forth the queer odor of burning petrol. Voices came from within this metal and glass box. Then the box stopped, only yards away from the kill. The voices inside were hushed. The noise and smell seemed to be over for the most part.

The lions hardly noticed. With faces covered in blood, panting heavily, and with strings of intestine stuck in their teeth, they continued the arduous and frenzied task of ripping the flesh off the zebra's bones. The lions were eating everything. The muscle, fat, gristle, bowels and ligaments were all consumed. If they were hungry enough, they would have even eaten the bones. Sometimes, when a human is eaten, only a heel bone or shoulder blade is left over.

Later, one would describe the scene as commonplace. Two men in a Land Rover. Ten lions eating their breakfast. Hyenas and vultures in the distance. A typical African morning.

Grass in Africa can grow up to six feet tall, making photography difficult. In the Land Rover, one man felt his classic photo was being ruined by the tall grass. He thought for a moment. He debated. Then he made a momentous decision. He opened the door of the vehicle and stepped down into the grass. He positioned himself five or six meters (approximately 16-20 feet) from the vehicle, camera in hand. His new position improved his view of the lions greatly. Little did he realize, though, that he had stepped down from the vehicle and onto the front page of every major South African daily newspaper.

Physically, man is no match for the lion. In a 100-meter race, the lion would cross the finish line in under four seconds, just as the fastest human reached the 30-meter mark. Only the cheetah is faster. With a running start a lion can jump over a 10-meter hole. Deadly accurate, lions have been known to bring down a Cape buffalo with one bite to the spine.

The lion can smell and hear far better than man. His coat makes him almost invisible in the grass. If he so desired, a lion could put two paws against any medium-sized automobile and turn it over. Seemingly the only advantage man has, besides intelligence, is that he sees color where the lion only sees black and white. But how comforting is it to know that you can see him in full color, as 500 pounds of pure carnivore streak towards you at 65 mph (115 kph). Three times faster than the fastest human, twice the size of a professional American football player, and practically invisible in his approach, the lion is a terrifying opponent.

Even the lion's black-and-white vision becomes an advantage. Diminished color gives him better vision at night, which is when lions do most of their hunting. They can see in only one-eighth the light that a human needs.

In the game park, the other man watched the lions from the Land Rover. The zebra kill fascinated him. With the camera perched on one knee and his eyes glued to the viewfinder, he stared at the scene. Soon he was clicking the shutter in fascination. He had never seen a kill before. Meanwhile, nearby in the grass, his friend knelt on one knee focusing his lens on the male of the pride whose wet, bloody face kept disappearing into the zebra carcass to rip away more flesh. He would come out for a moment, panting, chewing and swallowing. He seemed oblivious to the two men.

Then it happened. Perhaps a twig snapped. Perhaps the lioness growled. But suddenly the man's attention was riveted to his right. There, crouched low, was the lioness. The same grass which had hidden his view had also hidden her approach.

Staring at the man, the lioness kept her head low and tail against the ground. They stared at each other for a second which seemed like an eternity. His heart was pounding like a bass drum.

Then decidedly he started toward the car. The lioness was in the air in a flash, hitting him full force in the chest. Knocking him down hard, the lioness moved up towards his throat.

Experienced hunters know that once hit, your only hope is to feed the animal your hand and forearm. You can't fend him off completely, but perhaps a friend can fire a shot while the animal takes your wrist.

The man, however, did not think quickly. He only screamed as the jaws closed in on his throat. The lioness clamped down until he lost consciousness. He was dead before any help could arrive.

Inside the vehicle, his friend instinctively clicked the shutter, taking several pictures of the kill. These photos appeared in most of the major dailies in South Africa.

Popular culture warps our image of the lion. We see him in a zoo cage. We see Tarzan killing him in a movie. Our kids cuddle stuffed Simbas from Disney's *Lion King*. He becomes a harmless enigma in our minds. But to stand before the lion, eye to eye without bars, glass or fence, is absolutely horrifying. To hear him breathing, to feel his roar, is simply terrifying. But to be hunted is the sickest feeling of all. In the African savanna, you cannot outrun him, you cannot fight him, and you cannot hide. You are face to face with one of nature's most accomplished killers.

But this hunting scene is not limited to Africa. Spiritually, this scene occurs every day in every city, town and village in the world. As a Christian, you must realize you are being hunted. Satan, the lion, stalks you. He watches you. He is crouching nearby. You cannot run. You cannot hide. The absolute horror of facing the lion is unimaginable. However, one thing is guaranteed: You *will* be stalked. You *will* face him. You *will* grapple with him. I hope you are ready—for the fight of your life! Help is available. I pray this book will help you find it.

CHAPTER TWO

EVERYTHING, EVERY DAY, NEVER STOP

*For our struggle is not against flesh
and blood, but against the rulers, against the
authorities, against the powers of this dark
world and against the spiritual forces of evil
in the heavenly realms.*

EPHESIANS 6:12

he Great Commission is found in Matthew 28:18-20. Look carefully at the words of our Lord—so often quoted, yet so often misunderstood:

> Then Jesus came to them and said, "All authority in heaven and on earth has been given to me. Therefore go and make disciples of all nations, baptizing them in the name of the Father and of the Son and of the Holy Spirit, and teaching them to obey everything I have commanded you. And surely I am with you always, to the very end of the age."

Notice the simple commands: Go. Baptize. Teach everything.

How much should we teach the disciples after they are baptized? Everything that Jesus commanded. "Everything" encompasses a lot of material. If I'm going to baptize someone, then I should also stay with them and teach them to obey *everything*.

Notice that Jesus does not mention the teaching that the young disciple receives *before* baptism. When Jesus says to baptize them, he assumes we have already taught them his expectations of a disciple. Yet this intense instruction leading up to baptism is not even mentioned here. This verse is commanding the instruction necessary *after* baptism.

I have read the Great Commission many times, yet for years I missed this simple truth: Teach them everything!

"Everything" Means Everything

In the past, most of my discipling of young Christians involved getting together weekly, having some fun, discussing how they are doing and reading a scripture or two. Then perhaps we would pray. Obviously, all of this was and is good. Yet, Jesus calls us to go further. He did *not* disciple the Twelve in this manner. He taught them! He assumed nothing and taught them—everything!

"Everything" includes the Beatitudes, the Sermon on the Mount, Matthew 25 with its emphasis on caring for the poor, John 13 with its emphasis on being a servant, the parable of the unmerciful servant with its emphasis on forgiveness, and so on. We could say that this would include even those things that Jesus taught through the apostles and their work after his resurrection. This means everything in the letters of the New Testament. Since the New Testament calls us to study the Old Testament, this, too, must be taught to the new disciple. Let's be honest. While we have made great progress in our restoration of biblical one-on-one discipling, we still have many disciples who are fed far too much junk food instead of solid food.

We've all heard of such things as Lite Beer and Pepsi Lite. I believe that in many places, if Jesus took a hard look at the discipling going on, he might call it Discipleship Lite or Lite Love. "I tell you the truth," he might say. "This may taste great but it is not fulfilling!"

Obviously, the proof is in the pudding. Jesus discipled his apostles on a daily basis; he taught them to pray, preach, sacrifice and be humble. As we can tell from later writings and sermons, he obviously inspired them to study the Old Testament scriptures. And the fruit of his intense instruction? Only one of The Twelve fell away. The other eleven turned the world upside-down. After approximately thirty-six months with the Lord, they were publicly preaching and proving from the Old Testament that Jesus was the Messiah. We see Peter quoting extensively and without reservation from the Psalms and from Joel. It is incredible what Jesus did in such a short time with an uneducated, ordinary fisherman! Jesus used the Old Testament Scriptures, and he taught his disciples from the Law, the Prophets and the Psalms. We must do the same.

I meet many disciples who are thirty-six months old in the Lord, yet cannot quote from Joel. Sometimes, they haven't even read the book of Joel yet. And sadly, some cannot even find it in their Bibles. They are far from being able to prove Jesus is the Messiah exclusively from the Old Testament

We might hear Jesus say, "Hmmm...Discipleship Lite...half the calories."

So we must admit that while we have done well in teaching young disciples "something," we have not done well at all in teaching them "everything." Perhaps this lack of knowledge is a contributing factor in the hearts of people who leave the church within their first two years as disciples.

Daily Strengthening

The goal of the apostles in the first century was to teach their young converts everything Jesus had commanded. Acts 2:41 informs us that 3,000 young disciples were plopped down at the apostles' door barely seven weeks after Jesus had ascended back to heaven.

What were the apostles to do? Acts 2:46 spells it out: "Every day they continued to meet together...." Teaching, fellowship, prayer, wonders, miracles, selling of possessions and praise to God went on daily. Why? Because the apostles were feverishly trying to teach them to obey *everything*!

The apostle Paul voiced a similar attitude in Acts 20:31: "So be on your guard! Remember that for three years I never stopped warning each of you night and day with tears." The point is clear. The twelve best disciplers who ever lived worked on a *daily* basis to strengthen the young converts.

Recently I stood in front of a group of 150 disciples in South Africa. I asked the group how many

of them had met for prayer and Bible study once
a week for the last three weeks with their discipleship partner.

Sadly, not one hand went up. If you had been
there, would you have been the exception?

It is no surprise, therefore, that this ministry
group had actually shrunk during the year, despite
having baptized many people. I believe that's the
real fruit of Discipleship Lite.

Why don't we disciple people correctly? There
are a number of reasons, the top three of which I
want to discuss here.

First of all, we are lazy. It takes thought and
effort to prepare lessons and to follow up with
people. Visits, phone calls and conversations take
time. It may be cold or raining out. There's a good
show on television. Laziness creeps in like an in-
fectious disease.

Second, we can be prideful. It's glamorous to
baptize someone. Everyone's excited to see a
brand new baby Christian. People ask about them.
But because no one asks much about them after
baptism, we slack off on the instruction. "Everything, every day" becomes "a little something once
a week." And pretty soon we're not even meeting
together once a week.

The third reason, however, is the most important reason why we fail in teaching the young. We simply do not understand the spiritual battle which the young Christian faces. The devil is a roaring lion. He is a horrifying enemy. It is inevitable and unavoidable that the young Christian will be attacked by this spiritual killer. Rather than preparing them in advance for this encounter, we often skimp on their preparation and instruction. Then when the lion strikes, we immediately come to their assistance. We rush in with scriptures and advice. But we're too late. We should have been there long before the crisis with our scriptures and advice. We should have anticipated the lion! Now, all we can do is stand by and shout advice as the young disciple fights for his life.

Runners who don't train lose races. Students who don't study fail exams. Disciplers who don't teach their young Christians watch them get eaten alive by the lion.

Above all, understand the significance of this point. Don't wait for the crises before discipling the young Christian. Rather, assume the crises are coming, and work like mad to prepare for them *in advance.*

CHAPTER THREE

THE HORROR
OF BEING HUNTED

*...they will tear me like a lion
and rip me to pieces with no
one to rescue me.*

PSALM 7:2

With black-and-white vision the animal stared at the camp in front of him. Some ancient instinct told him to wait there. His tail occasionally jumped side to side. He felt the hunger growing within him. He would delay his attack only a little longer.

The disadvantage of being color-blind totally escaped the beast. Having never known color, he never missed it. He killed indiscriminately. Fur or skin color was not important to him. Whether the coat was striped like a zebra, golden brown like the impala or dirty gray like the warthog, it did not matter to him at all. And lately he had started hunting a new animal who came in several colors. To his color-blind eyes the prey sometimes appeared black or gray or even pale white. Yet inside, all those colors was the same juicy red flesh that he craved. Now he was hunting man.

And man was easy prey. Slow and weak, he had no long horns, claws or sharp teeth. The lion was now familiar with the human odor and associated that scent with a quick and simple dinner.

So there he sat, only 50 meters (95 yards) away from what to him must have seemed like a giant buffet table. He saw the campfire dying. He heard less and less conversation from within. Silently he rose and moved left to watch from a different angle. Not a twig snapped as he stealthily moved several paces. His padded feet and tan coat made him almost impossible to detect. He waited. Then all at once he stepped from the trees into the clearing. Five hundred pounds of hungry carnivore approached the crude fence surrounding the tents. It was time to kill. Although an assortment of smells bombarded him, he had singled out one particular scent which he now hunted. It beckoned him forward.

It had been a nerve wracking evening inside the camp. About fifty men—all from India—were sleeping in two cloth tents. The year was 1901 and they had come to Kenya to work on the new railroad connecting Mombasa to Lake Victoria.

Amazingly, the men were unarmed, but they had built a fence of woven thorn-tree branches which surrounded the camp. Stories of lions attacking the other camps terrified them, but they hoped the fence would deter any lion from entering the camp. In the end, the fence would only add to their horror.

It was well past midnight, and all of the exhausted workers were fast asleep as the lion crossed the clearing and approached the fence. He placed his paw on it and found it weak and wobbly. Then he shoved his body through a small hole just above ground level. The thorns cut into his flesh, but he ignored the pain. His hunger, as well as the scent, drove him onward.

With the fence now behind him he scanned the scene. Although it was very dark out, the camp was actually well lit for the lion. His eyes quickly identified the two cloth tents, a dying fire and a sleeping sentry. He stared at the man who was supposed to be on guard and listened to his snoring. The lion confidently approached.

Lions are picky eaters. The lion's hunger had been stirred by only one scent from the time he stood outside the camp. Fortunately for the guard, he was simply not on the menu that night. The lion left footprints only five feet from the sleeping man as he walked past.

His appetite drove him to the flap of the tent on the right. Inside he could smell what he so much desired. But ever cautious, he paused at the entrance and listened. Only the sounds of breathing and snoring came from within. The lion poked his head between two canvas sheets. He now looked around inside the tent. All appeared safe. His nose drove him straight ahead. Stepping over two lucky rail workers, he made his way to the poor soul whose smell had caught his fancy.

The lion had no respect for his prey. The humans had neither heard him enter nor smelled his presence. He sized up his prey. Biting down on the man's skull, he crushed the bones as if they were match sticks. The kill was instant. Blood spurted from the dead man's mouth and ears onto the sleeping men, waking them up as the lion dragged him across the tent. Twenty feet outside the tent, the lion began to eat, ripping into the stomach of the man, devouring the intestines and organs. Pressing his head into the chest cavity to rip away the soft flesh, the lion worked fast. His face was now covered with blood, which he licked off his fur with delight.

Inside the tent, the terrified workers, paralyzed with fear, heard the lion as he began to gnaw the bones. Cracking them in his mouth, the lion chewed and ate everything. He tore muscle from bone, and ligaments hung from his mouth, lodged in his teeth. He felt no fear, only his hunger. On other nights in other camps he had dragged bodies into the forest. Tonight he simply decided to eat inside the camp.

When something startled him, the beast raised his head. Then sinking his teeth deep into the corpse, he pulled himself and his prey through the fence and dragged the half-consumed carcass into the forest.

In the end, over a hundred workers would be eaten by the pride of eight lions. Terror reigned.

Lions are bold and courageous. But lions are also cautious and cunning. They may take hours in stalking their prey. They know that they can kill almost any animal they choose, yet they fear injury. Even a small gazelle can gore a lion, and an injury could render the lion unable to hunt. In pain he could not aggressively jostle for position at the next kill. An injury would diminish his speed and quickness. Indeed, an injury could lead to his own death because he does not hunt for sport; he hunts for survival.

I have seen lions hunting. They are territorial and will not follow the migrating herds. Rather, they hunt a specific area. When a herd moves near their region, they will approach slowly. They are keenly aware of wind direction and know how to stay downwind from their prey. But oftentimes they don't care if the herd is alerted—such is their confidence.

Frequently the lion will run at a herd. Not sprinting but just jogging, the lion will frighten the herd. His aim is to get them to move. He wants to see them run. To the human eye the herd's retreat seems normal enough. To the lion's sharp eye, dinner becomes very obvious. He notices who is old, who is tired or who is injured. A slight limp or any mannerism imperceptible to the human eye is obvious to the lion. He frightens the herd in order to spot the weak ones. Once he decides on his target, he will run past the others to get to his chosen prey.

Healthy impalas are fast. On a dry lake bed in Kenya they can reach speeds of over 72 kph (45 mph). Gazelle are even faster and the males have huge horns. The lions want none of this. It is too dangerous for them. Although fully capable of killing the strong, they prefer an easy kill—the weak and the wounded.

The healthy impala or zebra for the most part need fear the lion only if they separate themselves from the herd. The herd provides protection. It has an early warning system: one hundred eyes are better than two. But, pity the lone animal who stumbles upon a pride of lions. It is surely his last mistake.

All animals are at risk when they are young. Lions won't touch a full-grown elephant but they will eat a baby elephant if they can get it away from the herd. Indeed, animals must grow up quickly to survive in Africa. When a wildebeest is born, for instance, the young calf is up and standing within six minutes. He'll be running in only thirty minutes. The mother, as well, is virtually back to normal within seconds. Neither mother nor calf would survive even three hours of convalescing. If the lion, cheetah or leopard didn't get them, the hyenas would. It's amazing how God equips these animals to be up and moving almost instantly.

How horrible to be hunted by the lion. Yet how much more horrible to be devoured by him. Stay with the herd. Grow up quickly. Don't allow yourself to become weak or wounded. These are animal guidelines for survival in Africa.

Yet these are also God's guidelines for *your spiritual survival*. The Bible says that Satan, the spiritual lion is stalking you right now even as you read these pages.

Using persecution or peer pressure or negative media exposure or anything he can, the devil runs towards us. His purpose is to make us run. He wants to see who is weak, who is tired, who is hurt, who is alone. Then he attacks that individual. He attacks with intimidating roars and bloodcurdling charges. It is then, during the attack, that your discipling of the young Christian is revealed. If you have taught him well, he has a fighting chance. If you have neglected him, he will be dragged into the tall grass and eaten alive.

CHAPTER FOUR

A GUARANTEED APPOINTMENT

*For we are not
unaware of [Satan's] schemes.*

2 CORINTHIANS 2:11

atan, the roaring lion, is a cold and calculating killer. He is a dreadful and terrible opponent. Yet we are not helpless before him. We can protect ourselves from the spiritual murderer of our friends and loved ones. We can raise up strong disciples who will stand up to the devil. Yes, we can equip disciples to fight him successfully.

Indeed, we have no choice. The physical deaths described so far in this book are not nearly as gruesome as the suffering and torture to be endured in hell. As terrifying as it is to consider death at the jaws of a lion, it is even more terrifying to consider spiritual death in the bowels of hell.

Yet many of us seem to have forgotten the trials of the young Christian. We forget that the young are certain and easy targets for our enemy. We do not think about what it's like to be hunted, so our training of young disciples is slack.

Why did Jesus command us to teach the disciples *everything*? Why did the apostles gather the disciples *daily*? Why this feverish passion? Why this depth of preparation?

The reason for their intensity is that they were keenly aware of something many of us have forgotten: the enemy. The lion is coming. He will hunt and attack the young disciples. He cannot be bought, bribed, bargained with or deterred. No man can outrun him. He studies every weakness. And he will attack with fury and with an intent to kill.

The apostles knew this. Their love for the young church translated into intense preparation for the battles with Satan each disciple would face. Today, as disciples, we must imitate this conviction of the apostles. Often, too many disciples get too little help. When they come face to face with the lion, they are in a spiritual state of flabbiness and weakness. We try desperately to advise and counsel at that moment, but often it is too late.

Would a track coach begin to train the runner the day of the race? Would a teacher prepare the students only on test day? Would a soldier be instructed how to use his weapon while on the battlefield? Of course not! Yet this is exactly how so many of us disciple one another. We allow young Christians to face the devil with little or no preparation. Too many of us are "crisis disciplers." If there is a crisis, we march in to help with scriptures and counsel. We pat ourselves on the back because we "pulled the person through." But we were guaranteed beforehand that these attacks would come. Perhaps it would not have been a crisis at all if we had prepared and trained the young Christian in advance!

"Building" images in the New Testament teach us some important lessons relating to the challenges we are discussing. In many passages, Christians are collectively compared to a building. In 1 Corinthians 3:10-15, the apostle Paul compares converting disciples to Christ to constructing a building. Helping people not only become Christians but to remain in the faith is a lot like building a sound structure.

"For no one can lay any foundation other than

the one already laid, which is Jesus Christ" (1 Corinthians 3:11). Paul says that Jesus Christ is the only foundation. Our relationship with God, our convictions about Jesus—these are the building blocks which must support our faith. If our faith rests just on the inspiring sermons of the preacher, the fired-up singing or the warm fellowship in the church, then eventually we will stumble and fall spiritually. Each of these things is good and important; but they cannot be substituted for Jesus as a foundation. Knowing Jesus Christ through deep, personal Bible study and prayer is the only foundation that will ever stand against the storms.

This principle must be reflected in my discipling of young Christians. There have been discipleship times when I've spent "fun time" (pizza and basketball) and "discussion time" (a short, hurried "How are you doing?"). This was my idea of discipling. I would address major problems only when they arose. I did not build on the Jesus foundation. I did not give the detailed instruction and teaching from the Scriptures like Jesus did. So when the lion came, what I had done was not enough. When the lion attacked, the young disciples were hurt and fell because I failed to prepare them in advance for the challenges.

I shared the Bible with Bill (not his real name) in New York City. We studied the Scriptures two or three times per week and Bill was truly excited when he become a Christian. After his baptism, I remember how he brought five or six friends weekly to study the Bible. Bill and I would get together for our weekly "How are you?" talks as well. But sadly, all we ever did was talk. We never opened up the Bible again to study. Before his conversion we studied constantly. Afterwards, I left his spiritual development to the church lessons and his own private study. When the lion came, he was easy prey.

I know that Bill will stand before God on his own and that he must take responsibility for his own choices. Yet I know now that I could have done much more in preparing him to stand firm and faithful and to fight.

If any man builds on this foundation using gold, silver, costly stones, wood, hay or straw, his work will be shown for what it is, because the Day will bring it to light. It will be revealed with fire, and the fire will test the quality of each man's work (1 Corinthians 3:12-13).

If you do a lousy job in building, then that will be exposed—the building will fall. But if you build with solid materials, then the building will stand.

But notice what Paul guarantees. Your work *will* be shown for what it is. Fire *will* test the quality of each man's work. Not just on Judgment Day, but also in this life. The shocking truth is that every disciple will be tested—tested with fire. We must not wait for the actual flames in order to get serious about fireproofing the building!

After I became a Christian, many tests came my way. Satan came not like a match, but like a blowtorch. After my baptism, suddenly old girlfriends appeared looking for sex. Old friends appeared, as well, wanting to go to bars and clubs. Some friends ridiculed my decision. A few ceased to even be my friends. It was a lonely and difficult time. I had no concept of how the lion hunted. He was approaching me, making me run, watching me move. He wanted to see if I would waver, weaken or tire. He looked for my weaknesses. There was talk of nice job offers in cities where I knew there were no strong ministries. Satan's fire tested every joint, beam and brick in the structure. Praise God that I stood strong. Yes, I have some scorch marks. Yes, I made some mistakes. But I'm still standing firm, and I believe that I'm stronger for the testing.

I thank God especially for the men who helped me during that time. Their names may not mean much to you, but I owe them my life. Mitch Mitchell, Gary Hundly and Gary Knutson taught and strengthened me on various occasions as I was stalked by the lion in my early days. They did not want to just watch a video or eat pizza. They built with "gold, silver and costly stones" in order to fireproof the building. Their instruction and preparation meant my survival in those early days when I faced the lion.

Let us put an end to the weekly and "weakly" Discipleship Lite. Let us not be guilty of intense Bible study before baptism followed by neglect of the Bible afterwards. The Bible compares the care of young Christians to raising a child (1 Thessalonians 2), building a building (1 Corinthians 3:9-15), and feeding a family (1 Corinthians 3:1-2). All of these activities are *daily*, not weekly. With proper training, we can help each other to stand up to the lion. "Resist the devil, and he will flee from you!" (James 4:7).

CHAPTER FIVE

THE BEATING
OF YOUR LIFE

*"...woe to the earth and the sea,
because the devil has gone down to you!
He is filled with fury,
because he knows that his time is short."*

REVELATION 12:12

Jesus was constantly impressing upon his disciples the importance and reality of the spiritual world. He was constantly trying to make heaven and hell, angels and demons, and God and Satan real to his disciples. Having come from eternity into our world of time and space, Jesus knew well the reality of the spiritual realm. Christianity is not just a philosophy for living, but a clear and telling view of the unseen world. Today as you read these words, you are being watched by your enemy. His aliases are numerous and varied: the devil, Satan, Beelzebub, Lucifer, the beast, the prince of darkness, the lion. He schemes (2 Corinthians 2:11). He is filled with fury (Revelation 12:12). He hates you. And he watches.

He watches your young brothers and sisters, as well. He sees them when they wake in the morning. He notices the long prayer with sadness. He feels God's presence growing stronger in response. Yet he also notices with delight the ever-shrinking Bible study. He sees how this young Christian is growing lazy in his reading of the Scriptures. Many days he sees him choose sleep over Bible study. And although the disciple may not even admit it to himself yet, the lion takes note.

Is it time to strike? No, not yet.

The lion waits for the opportune time.

The beast watches the Christian at church. He's singing and enjoying the fellowship. "Not good," the lion thinks. But he is heartened to see that his prey cannot find the books in the Bible. "I've got one," he thinks. "Two months old in the Lord, and he does not understand the importance of the sword he holds."

Now a scheme begins to form in his mind. Christians are starting to neglect the young disciple. No one is calling. No one is having great talks with him anymore. He may look happy on the outside, but the beast knows he is limping. The beast coldly views him like a sick zebra wandering from the herd.

His plan is simple yet tailored with this prey in mind. When the young Christian arrives at work, there's a note from an old girlfriend or maybe a lustful wink from a coworker.

Now the lion strikes, tempting him with corporal pleasures he's only dreamed of before. Now is the time when the young disciple needs scriptures about purity and conviction written on his heart. Now they could be used powerfully to fight. Sadly, the man is as defenseless as he is ignorant. To the lion the weakness is obvious. The outcome is almost inevitable. The man chooses pleasure over God. It is a gradual process, but soon he is avoiding the church services. He stops praying. He won't even talk to his friends. Eventually, his spiritual heart stops beating altogether. On that day, some disciples have a pizza and watch a video, but the lion believes he had the better meal. He smiles and moves on to stalk his next victim.

Caring for young Christians is a great and heavy responsibility. We must equip them to fight spiritually. We must anticipate the attack. We must help them to be strong *before* the lion pounces.

In Matthew 7:24-27, Jesus describes two types of builders. The wise man builds his house on the rock. This is the man who hears Jesus' message and puts it into practice. The foolish builder builds his house on the sand. This is the man who hears Jesus' message but does not put what he hears into practice. When the storms come and beat upon the buildings, the wise man's house stands. The foolish man's house falls.

Although the men described are very different, they have one thing in common. Both men received a horrendous beating. One stood. One fell.

Several years ago I spoke with a Christian in New York City who was going to have to testify in a trial. It was a sad story which he recounted. He was standing on a concrete train platform one day when he witnessed a small man insulting a much larger man. The larger man grabbed him and threw him to the ground. Cupping the small man's head in his hands, the larger man pounded his head against the rock-hard pavement. He pounded the man relentlessly, until the back of the man's head was soft and mushy. Blood ran down the platform. The small man lay limp in his hands and died moments later. My friend had seen it all.

This chilling scene reminded me of the lives of young Christians. They are beaten upon! Satan pounds them relentlessly. He's merciless. It's horrifying. His punches are deadly temptations. His blows are devastating trials. His club is persecution. The fight is on!

The questions for everyone who cares for new Christians are: Are you preparing your friend for this beating? Are you building their strength with solid food (1 Corinthians 3)? Are you striving to teach them everything (Matthew 28)? Are you readying them for the brutal battle which God guarantees will take place?

Or are you lazy, feeding them videos and pizza instead of God's word? Are you too tired to call, too busy to visit or too preoccupied to remember? Will your laziness result in totally unskilled disciples facing a merciless, brutal killer?

Wake up! The spiritual war is real. The battle is real. The casualties are real. Truly the Scriptures use shocking images to wake us up.

The fires, the lion and the beatings describe a reality to which many of us are oblivious. We don't see the lion. We've forgotten the fires. We've forgotten the horror of being hunted and beaten.

The need of the hour is not to feel guilty. Rather, we must feel indignant. So you want to disciple a young Christian? Then realize you are not just signing up for a weekly appointment. You're volunteering to train them and equip them for the fight of their lives. New disciples need your help, advice, prayers and counsel. Don't give them orders or boss them around. You're not Jesus. Rather, help them to prepare for the trials and battles that are coming their way! Let the Scriptures ring in your ears as you love your new brothers and sisters. Words like "everything," "every day," "met together daily," "the lion," "fires," "beaten" need to be written on your heart.

At this point someone might ask, "The message here is that we should help the weak, right?" No. The point is not to help just the weak. Everyone should know that they should help the weak. Rather, the point I am making here is to urgently prepare both weak and strong alike for the fires of testing that are coming. Don't let the lion sneak up on your brothers and sisters. Rather, prepare them.

First, take them deeper into the Scriptures. The deeper into God's word you both delve, the better. Help them to understand the miracles, parables and messages of Jesus. Teach them about the Pentateuch, the major and minor prophets, as well as the epistles. Teach them about evidences, church history and your own favorite passages. The deeper you go, the less vulnerable they will be to Satan's vicious attack.

Second, take them with you. Challenging someone to evangelize and pray daily can be daunting indeed. It's like telling a six-year-old to paint a masterpiece painting or to learn to swim in thirty minutes. They see you do it, but that does not mean they can do it themselves. So you must walk with them. Give gentle suggestions. Praise every victory. Help them by going with them. Too many of us say "what" without showing "how."

Third, get your own life in order. You must be having quiet times in order to share from those quiet times. You must be evangelizing personally in order to teach someone how. People will not do what you say. They will do what you *do*. Make sure your own example is an inspiration to them.

Fourth, pray. Pray hard. Pray like crazy. Paul asked the Romans "to join me in my struggle by praying to God for me" (Romans 15:30). Join in the struggle which confronts the young Christian. Do it by praying.

Finally, become indignant. And from this indignation, may a spring of love, help and concern well up and flow into the lives of young Christians everywhere.

The lion is coming. Prepare *now*. When he arrives is too late to begin.

CHAPTER SIX

VICTORY AT
KRUGER PARK

*[Jesus] replied, "I saw Satan fall
like lightning from heaven."*

LUKE 10:18

arry Wolhuter had finished his day's patrol in South Africa's Kruger Park and was now headed home. It was a cool winter's evening in August of 1903, and Wolhuter, a game ranger in the world-famous game park, rode his horse ahead of his other companions accompanied by his faithful dog, Bull. He knew the area well, and he loved being under the stars.

He looked forward to the ride at the end of his hard day. He was tired and thirsty, but six miles ahead was his camp and a water hole. He felt himself unwind and begin to relax and enjoy the scenery as his horse carried him homeward.

The grass in August is brown and brittle. Often it catches on fire, with the small bush fires leaving black patches in its wake. Wolhuter passed through patches of tall dead grass, followed by areas of burned scorched earth.

Ahead he heard some rustling in the grass. Suspecting it might be an antelope of some kind (reedbuck he guessed), he waited for the animals to sprint away into the night. But as he advanced, he saw no movement. The night was dark, and he peered hard into the grass and shrubs ahead of him. The night plays tricks on your eyes, and as the horse moved slowly ahead, the two bushes began to transform. He was only ten feet away when his brain finally interpreted the scene in front of him. Those were not two bushes. Those were two male lions, crouched and ready to spring.

There was no time to draw his rifle. In desperation he pulled the reins, trying to turn the horse. Just as he turned his back on the animals, Wolhuter felt the staggering impact of a lion slamming into both his back and the horse's rump. Immediately the horse reared, sending the rifle spinning off into the night, the lion to the left, and Wolhuter to the right. He landed in a heap on the grass below, stunned by the impact.

He could not see the lion. In fact, there was no time to look. Wolhuter had fallen practically on top of the second lion, who had been heading for the horse's neck. This lion simply made a slight course correction and bit down hard into Wolhuter's right shoulder. The fangs sunk deep into his flesh, locking onto his shoulder and arm like a trap.

David Livingston wrote that while he was being bitten by a lion, he felt no pain. A vague numbness, perhaps. Wolhuter, however, felt excruciating pain shoot through his body as the lion bit down. It seemed that every nerve cell in his body exploded in torment. And to make matters worse, the lion was not going to eat him just then. The beast began to drag him along the path.

The horse, meanwhile, had galloped away with the other lion in hot pursuit with the dog following behind. Wolhuter was left alone in the jaws of his killer.

As the lion dragged Wolhuter down the path, his mind raced to find any possible plan of attack. He had heard the old wives' tale that if you punched a lion in the nose, then he would drop whatever was in his mouth and sneeze. But he quickly realized that the lion would only pick him up again, probably by biting his head.

Wolhuter was truly in a predicament. His right shoulder was locked in the lion's teeth. The lion was pulling him down the path with his legs and back dragging on the ground under the lion's body. His face was shoved into the animal's foul-smelling mane. His worst fear was that the lion would start to eat him while he was still alive.

Suddenly he remembered his knife. A six-inch blade, it was sheathed to his right hip. He wondered whether it was in the holster at all, since it had fallen out on previous outings. With his right arm totally useless, he began to bring his left arm around his back to feel if the knife was there. It was. He grabbed the handle, as intense pain rushed like waves through his body. Almost miraculously, he unsheathed it and pulled it around to his left side.

He knew he would have only one or two chances to stab the lion. He could not afford to simply hurt him. He must find his heart and seriously wound him. As he gripped the knife, he felt with his hand for the proper spot on the lion's chest.

With all of his fading strength he stabbed the lion in what he hoped was the heart. The blade sunk in deep. Withdrawing it quickly, he stabbed again. The lion made a noise and dropped him on the ground. Quickly he slashed the lion's throat, feeling the warm blood flow onto his arm and chest. Amazingly, the lion stumbled away to lie down, leaving Wolhuter in the path. The game warden staggered to his feet shouting choice expressions at the lion who slunk under a shrub.

It was at this moment that he remembered the second lion. He knew the lion would come back. So, Wolhuter moved toward a tree and with only one arm managed to climb up twelve feet and wedge himself between two branches. Sure enough, within moments the lion returned. While the first lion lay dying in the grass, the second came slowly down the path sniffing the man's blood. He reached the point where the lion's blood went one way and the man's blood the other way. He followed the man's blood to the base of the tree. Standing up, the lion put two paws on the tree and growled low. Wolhuter knew this was it. If he could climb this tree with one arm, then certainly the lion could climb it (or at the least, shake him loose). He racked his brain in the darkness, but nothing came to mind.

It was this moment that his dog, Bull, arrived. He immediately sicced him on the lion. The dog managed to hold the lion off for almost an hour, until the rest of the party finally arrived. Lighting a bonfire to keep the lion away, the rescuers pulled Wolhuter out of the tree. It would be a five-day trek to the hospital. But ultimately Wolhuter would survive the bite and the terrible infection. Even though his right arm was severely and permanently damaged, he still considered himself lucky. He not only continued to work as the game warden, but he lived another 60 years to tell the tale. The dead lion was skinned and hung in his home.

So you want to disciple someone? I have spent the better part of this book trying to frighten you into action. If we do nothing to protect ourselves and others, then the killing will continue. But if we follow God's plan and Jesus' example in discipling, we can send the lion scurrying away.

Harry Wolhuter has shown us that the lions of Africa are not invincible. In a similar way, as frightening as our spiritual enemy may be, disciples of Jesus are well equipped to defeat him. Indeed, let me go one step further. It is not the lion who is invincible. As Christians, if we trust God and imitate Jesus, then it is *we* who are invincible.

CHAPTER SEVEN

VICTORY IN JESUS

The reason the Son of God appeared was to destroy the devil's work.

1 JOHN 3:8B

The sun was setting on another Nairobi day. The day's heat was fading, but this was little consolation for the commuters stuck in the choking traffic. Shem sat in his car on Ngong Road, inching home. It was a nice car. Not brand new, but it ran well. He glanced over at the *matatu* (bus) next to him. En route to some of the outer neighborhoods, it was packed like a sardine can. As traffic moved along, Shem thought about how far he had come in Kenya.

Nairobi has a 40% unemployment rate. Those who do work earn only $30 to $100 (US) a month. Thousands live in despair and hopelessness. But not Shem. Shem had "arrived." He was driving his own car to his own house on his own plot of land. There waiting for him was his supper, being served by his pretty wife on their finest tableware. Shem's business was doing so well, he even had a phone installed in his house. Just think what the guys back in the village would say about that! Not only did he have a phone, but it worked. Life was good.

Shem enjoyed going to the horse-racing track on weekends. Sometimes he would win. Often he would lose. But that was okay; he could afford it. As time passed, however, he became a more accomplished gambler. He knew many of the horses and jockeys, and would occasionally hit it big. He had arrived, he thought.

It began at work—late in the day. His eyes seemed to have trouble focusing. Soon he had trouble seeing even when he wasn't tired. Routine things became a problem for Shem as his sight diminished. Night driving, reading and spotting things at a distance all became nearly impossible. Later he described his experience: "It was like milk being poured slowly into water." Shem was going blind. He tried going to doctors for help, but they could neither cure nor slow his fading vision. He was afraid. Kenya has no social security or disability programs.

His whole life began to unravel right in front of him. The first thing he lost was his car. Unable to drive anymore, Shem sold it and began to take the bus instead. Work became more and more difficult. His trusted employees were stealing from him, and Shem simply could not run his shop effectively anymore. As his business fell apart, so did his ability to pay his bills. Money was tighter and tighter. He lost his phone. He lost his house. Worst of all he lost his wife. It was absolutely the lowest point in his life. He had "arrived" at a place he did not want to be. He had lost it all.

Blind, bitter and dejected, Shem moved into a sprawling slum in Nairobi called Kibera. Here approximately 300,000 of East Africa's poorest try to get on their feet in the big city. Police protection is a joke, there is no rubbish removal, and the sanitation system consists of carrying a bucket from your house out to the ditch that runs down the road. Approximately every twenty houses have a low-pressure water tap between them and water lines often run beside or across open sewage ditches. This contributes to the massive outbreak of diseases from time to time. Except for the drug pushers who may have cellular phones, Kibera has no electricity or telephone service.

Shem's only hope seemed to be the race track. Reduced to living in squalor, he eked out an existence helping bettors. He would advise gamblers on the best bets, then he would simply wait for a tip or gift afterward. It was his only means of survival.

In Africa the only social security system is the extended family, and Shem's family had rejected him after he lost his sight. For him, life had taken a cruel and bitter turn. He was an old blind man barely surviving.

The path outside Shem's little house was not paved so it turned into a muddy mess each time it rained. Raw sewage ran through an open ditch outside his door. The walls of his home were made of mud. The floor was mud. The solitary window had no glass panes and the roof was a single sheet of corrugated tin. Hot as fire in the sun and deafening in the rain, the house could also be quite chilly at night. Yet, Shem locked the rickety door with a small padlock each time he left.

His furniture consisted of an old army cot and a simple stove. Each time he cooked, the whole place would fill with smoke. He had to walk down the path to the tap closest to his home to draw water. Shem had a few shirts and pairs of trousers he hung on a nail. Threadbare and torn, one last suit jacket was all that remained of a moderately prosperous past he once knew. Sometimes overwhelmed, Shem would just sit on the army cot and weep. Tears would fall from his blind eyes to the dirty floor as he tried to make sense of it all. He knew what it was to be in darkness.

One day early in 1990, Shem was met by disciples and invited to a group Bible discussion. Not particularly religious, he attended mostly out of curiosity. As the discussion progressed, he found himself comforted and intrigued by the Jesus he discovered in the Bible. Soon he was studying the Bible with a disciple named Richard Alawaye on a regular basis.

In July of 1990, Shem stepped out of spiritual darkness by being baptized into Christ. It was a glorious day, but it was only the beginning. Immediately the lion began to stalk him. Infuriated by the loss of his subject, the enemy hungered to reclaim Shem with a vengeance. He watched the young blind Christian closely with steely black-and-white vision to uncover every weakness.

The brothers close to Shem were not blind to Shem's spiritual state, however. They had a healthy respect for the lion and knew he would strike soon. They knew the attack was unavoidable and inevitable. They knew the clock was ticking. Shem, like any young Christian, must get up quickly on his young spiritual legs and run with the herd. Fortunately, he was excited about the help he received. Having been abandoned by his relatives, he was amazed by the love and care of his new brothers in Christ.

The brothers were both sacrificial and resourceful. It must have shocked the lion every morning to watch Christians come to Shem's house to read the Scriptures to him. Shem listened attentively. He memorized passages. He discussed God's word in depth with the brothers both morning and evening. His Bible knowledge sprinted forward at an accelerated rate.

Shem needed help getting on the bus and into town for church services, so every Sunday and Wednesday, a fellow disciple would lend a hand to lead him to church. But not only that—Shem would initiate times to go out sharing his faith with the brothers. Holding on to their hands, he walked through the crowded neighborhoods speaking to whoever would listen to him. He brought many people to church with him. He studied the Bible with them and baptized many of them.

I met Shem late in 1990 when my family and I moved to Nairobi. I led a Bible discussion group in Kibera and went there daily to evangelize. Kibera was not filled with Kenya's richest and brightest. It was filled with the huddled masses struggling to survive. And yet it was there that I learned about Africa.

Before I spoke Swahili, Shem would often translate for me. We would talk late into the night about life in Africa. We'd eat *dengu* and *chapati* while we discussed witchcraft, polygamy, tribalism and government corruption. We would go out to street preach. Our routine was rather unique. I would begin in English with a Swahili translator. A crowd would always gather. Then we would switch. I would speak Swahili and the brother would translate into English. People would be shocked. They were stunned that the *mzungu* (white man) would come to Kibera and speak their language.

Thanks be to God and to the love and determination of the brothers in Kibera, Shem grew quickly. Although we urge in Africa that every disciple receive a thirty-minute weekly Bible study from their discipler, the brothers went far beyond this. They loved him and discipled him as Jesus would have. So against all odds, Shem rose up and became a pillar in the Kibera ministry. Starting with only four Christians, within three years they grew to 150 disciples.

Shem can still be seen in Kibera today. Accompanied by one of the Christians, he walks the dusty pathways between the huts inviting people to Bible discussions. He now leads two Bible discussion groups. Since he's never been able to use notes because of his blindness, he simply speaks from his heart. His Bible knowledge has become formidable. One night he asked for Psalm 51 to be read. When the Christian started reading, Shem held up his hand. "Hold up," he said, "that's Psalm 52. I asked for Psalm 51." Although Shem may be old and blind, he's still as sharp as a tack and the Scriptures are written on his heart and mind.

I believe the lion never came close to a victory with Shem. Oh yes, he had his struggles. But because the brothers close to Shem loved him so deeply, Shem grew stronger and stronger. Brothers like Joseph and Caxton who discipled Shem followed the Bible's simple instructions. *Every day* they strove to teach Shem *everything* Jesus had commanded.

Sometime, you'll get to meet Shem in heaven if you don't meet him here. Obviously he's excited to go there. Although he's been a Christian for years, he's never seen a Christian's face. He's never seen the faces of the brothers who've protected him from the lion. But he has seen and felt their deep love. And I suppose that's all that matters.

As powerful as the lion can be and as weak and vulnerable as man can appear, the lion cannot stop the disciple. The lion cannot stop one who is filled with the Holy Spirit, who is armed with the word of God and who is surrounded by his brothers or sisters. Though the lion is mighty, Jesus is greater.

EPILOGUE

hen I first wrote this book, I had no idea the way the enemy was plotting to attack me. After turning this material over to my publisher, I received some very bad news at a hospital in Johannesburg. "You have cancer," said the doctor, "and we need to operate tomorrow." I was in shock over the news, scarcely understanding the magnitude of it all. As I sat on the hospital bed, thoughts flooded my mind. What about my wife? And my three children? What if I die? This just was not supposed to be happening.

The next three months brought with it a host of frightening experiences. I had two operations, dozens of shots and x-rays, and four weeks of radiation therapy. It was a challenging time for me, but I was driven to hold on to God's hand as never before. I know the lion was watching. I am confident that he crouched nearby and studied me closely for any weaknesses. I know he saw many.

At times I was afraid. Other times I was worried or anxious. On several occasions I cried. Cancer is not just about being ill. Cancer is a challenge to keep the faith under pressure.

As a Christian, however, my defenses against the lion were far stronger than I realized. My wife stood by me like a rock. Dear friends, Steve Johnson and Steve Kinnard, traveled to South Africa from New York just to encourage me. I received flowers, cards and calls from Christians around the world telling me that they were praying for me daily. I wasn't just moved; I was astonished! All these prayers made me a much more confident and joyful cancer patient than I could have ever hoped.

More than ever, I realized how important it is for every disciple to have strong friendships within God's kingdom. When the lion came to my door, my brothers and sisters rallied to my side. Every disciple needs close friends, because friendship helps defeat the lion.

The lion is one of the most impressive of all God's creatures and has captured man's imagination since the earliest times. Some biblical passages use the lion in a metaphorical way to illustrate God's courage, power and supremacy (for examples see Isaiah 31:4; Jeremiah 49:19; Amos 3:7-8). Jesus is even described in the Book of Revelation as the Lion of the tribe of Judah (Revelation 5:5). But there are other characteristics of the lion that cause the Bible to describe our enemy the devil as a roaring lion, seeking whom he may devour. It is this image that I have tried to present as powerfully and persuasively as possible. Until we understand and have deep conviction about this idea, brothers and sisters of ours will continue to be easy victims of a cunning and powerful opponent.

During the last two years, we have stressed the behavior of the lion in the Johannesburg church. Again and again we have reminded the church that Satan is a horrible and merciless enemy, that young disciples will face him and that we must prepare one another now for the unavoidable trials which are coming.

As a church we have changed. We have repented of the neglect so often characteristic of our past discipleship. We have committed ourselves to the serious task of equipping young disciples in their struggle with the beast.

Yes, some still wander from the faith in Johannesburg. But far fewer wander than before. God has blessed the church. Whether in the microcosm of my own struggle with cancer or the broad scope of the Johannesburg congregation, we've seen victories.

But this is not a time to relax or rest. A whole new generation of young disciples have been baptized. Like the mother wildebeest helping her young on the African plains, we must help these young disciples to get on their feet quickly. Just over there in the grass crouches the lion in waiting. With coldhearted attentive eyes he watches our every move. And he will be watching us closely till the very end of the age. I pray my words make him more real to you. I pray that you realize that in Jesus Christ we can always defeat him. I pray you will prepare everyone you love for his certain attacks.

Bibliography

Capstick, Peter Hathaway. *Death in the Silent Places.* New York:
    St. Martin's Press, 1981.

Patterson, J.H. *The Man-Eaters of Tsavo.* New York:
    St. Martin's Press, 1986.
    (Originally published: London: Macmillian, 1907).

Wolhuter, Harry. *Memories of a Game Ranger.* Johannesburg:
    Wildlife Protection Society of South Africa,1948.

About the Author

Mike Taliaferro and his wife, Anne-Brigitte, lead a multiracial church of nearly 1500 disciples in Johannesburg, South Africa. He and Anne-Brigette have planted and led churches in South America and Africa. In 1987 they moved from New York City to Sao Paulo, Brazil, and planted the church there that now numbers over 1300 disciples. In 1989 they were asked to focus their efforts on the continent of Africa where they planted churches in Harare, Zimbabwe, and Abidjan, Ivory Coast. In 1991 they moved to Nairobi, Kenya, where they led the church in that city. They have been in Johannesburg since 1992 directing efforts to evangelize all of Africa with the gospel of Jesus Christ.

Mike and Anne-Brigette are bold and inspirational leaders and powerful speakers. Their passion for the gospel and for people is contagious. They lead one of the most remarkable churches in the world at one of the most unique times in South African history. This will surely be the first of many great books that will grow out of their work.

The Taliaferros have three children: Matthew, 7, Nathan, 5, Joshua, 3.

OTHER BOOKS FROM DPI

The Victory of Surrender
by Gordon Ferguson

In *The Victory of Surrender,* Gordon Ferguson shares with the reader his own spiritual journey, showing how he and all of us tend to be "god players" and how we resist the idea of surrendering to God's will. While surrender goes against the grain of natural thinking, Gordon shows how, in situation after situation, it is the only path to peace, security and victory.

Also available is *The Victory of Surrender Study Guide* which gives direction for thirty days of mediation on this great theme. Nothing frustrates the enemy you have just read about any more than a surrendered life.

The Victory of Surrender
220-page paperback $10.99
Study Guide $3.99

True and Reasonable
by Douglas Jacoby

In a skeptical age we need solid reasons for faith. In this book, Douglas Jacoby provides these as he addresses the existence of God, the reliability of the Bible, the resurrection of Jesus and a number of other topics. A specialist in the field of Christian evidences, the author helps readers see that faith in God, Jesus Christ and the Bible is no blind leap into the dark.

True and Reasonable
109-page paperback $5.99

Mind Change: The Overcomer's Handbook
by Thomas A. Jones

The enemy tries to use illness, losses, trials, disappointments, fears and opposition to discourage, frighten and defeat disciples. But none of these things surprise God. He has a plan for us to overcome them all. Written by DPI's managing editor out of his own challenge with multiple sclerosis, this book you will help you see that your challenges are not unique and that God's plan for overcoming will work for you.

Mind Change: The Overcomer's Handbook
160-page hardback (gift edition) $10.99
160-page paperback $7.99

The Unveiling
by Curt Simmons

Nothing helps a disciple in his battle against Satan like a right understanding of God. In this book, Curt Simmons seeks to lift the veils that keep us from seeing God clearly. In a unique style that blends frequent references to pop culture with poignant biblical insights, the author shows the real God of the Bible.

The Unveiling
202-page paperback $10.99

Prices subject to change

Life to the Full
A study of the writings of James, Peter, John and Jude
by Douglas Jacoby

Raising Awesome Kids in Troubled Times
by Sam and Geri Laing

Let It Shine: A Devotional Book for Teens
edited by Thomas and Sheila Jones

She Shall Be Called Woman
Volume I: Old Testament Women
edited by Sheila Jones and Linda Brumley

She Shall Be Called Woman
Volume II: New Testament Women
edited by Sheila Jones and Linda Brumley

The Disciple's Wedding
by Nancy Orr with Kay McKean

For information about ordering these
and many other resources from DPI, call
1-800-727-8273
or from outside the U.S.
617-938-7396
or write to
DPI, One Merrill Street, Woburn, MA 01801-4629